BURGESS, MERCHANT AND PRIEST

Perth Market, late 15th century

CHRISTINA UNWIN

Burgess, Merchant and Priest

Burgh Life in the Scottish Medieval Town

Derek Hall

Series editor: Gordon Barclay

BIRLINN LTD
with
HISTORIC SCOTLAND

THE MAKING
OF SCOTLAND

Series editor:
Gordon Barclay

Other titles available:

First published in Great Britain in 2002 by Birlinn Ltd,
West Newington House, 10 Newington Road, Edinburgh EH9 1QS
www.birlinn.co.uk

Copyright © Derek Hall 2002
Illustrations © individuals and organisations as credited
Maps © Historic Scotland

British Library Cataloguing in Publication Data
A catalogue record for this book is available on request from the British Library

ISBN 1 84158 147 X

Series Design:
James Hutcheson

Design:
Christina Unwin

Printed and bound by
Book Print S.L.

Contents

Location Map

Kirkwall (1486)

Tarbert (1329)

Cromarty (pre 1264?)
Dingwall (1226/7)
Rosemarkie (1214 x 1286)
Nairn (1190)
Elgin (1130 x 1153)
Cullen (1189 x 1198)
Banff (1189 x 1198)
Forres (1130 x 1153)
Auldearn (1179 x 1182)
Inverness (1130 x 1153)
Fyvie (Pre 1264)

Kintore (1187 x 1200)
Aberdeen (1124 x 1153)

Inverbervie (1341)
Forfar (1153 x 1162)
Montrose (1124 x 1153)

Perth (1152 x 1153)
Cupar (1327)
Auchterarder (1246)
Falkland (1458)
Crail (1178)
Clackmannan (1153 x 1164)
Dunfermline (1124 x 1127)
Stirling (1124 x 1127)
Kinghorn (1165 x 1172)
Airth (1195 x 1203)
Burntisland (1541)
Dumbarton (1222)
Linlithgow (1138)
Inverkeithing (1153 x 1162)
Kirkintilloch (pre 1211)
Edinburgh (1124 x 1127)
Haddington (1124 x 1153)
Renfrew (1124 x 1127)
Glasgow
Rothesay (1400/1401)
Rutherglen (1175 x 1178)
Berwick-upon-Tweed (1119 x 1124)
(1124 x 1153)
Lanark (1153 x 1159)
Peebles (1152 x 1153)
Selkirk (pre 1328)
Roxburgh (1119 x 1124)
Ayr (1203 x 1206)
Jedburgh (1159 x 1165)

New Galloway (1630)
Dumfries (1186)
Wigtown (pre 1292)
Kirkcudbright (pre 1341)

0 10 20 30 40 50 60 70 80 Km
0   10   20   30   40   50 Miles

Background

This is the story of the creation of the modern Scottish town. Scotland was never settled by the Romans, therefore, unlike England, the idea of the town is a late development. A total of 197 burghs of different types were founded in Scotland between the 12th and 17th centuries. This book will try to show what we have learned about some of these burghs over the last 25 years, largely through the results of archaeological excavation. The information uncovered by these excavations allows us to describe the different facets of medieval urban life, and to show how cosmopolitan many of the burghs were.

We did not know much about them, however, until the 1970s when urban archaeology in Scotland took off. The first major excavations were carried out in advance of urban regeneration in Elgin, Aberdeen, Perth and St Andrews. Modern conservation policies now ensure that major building projects are unlikely to take place in the cores of historic burghs. There are some exceptions however. The recent excavations at the new site of the Scottish Parliament in Edinburgh, for example, probably represent the largest urban excavation ever undertaken in Scotland.

Perth High Street Excavations 1975
General view, looking south.
SUAT LTD

Scottish Antiquarians

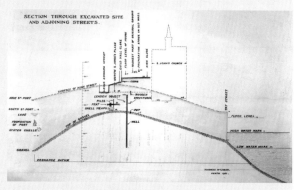

Archaeological Deposits
Drawing by Thomas McLaren of archaeological deposits revealed by construction work in Perth 1921.

Interest in antiquities was very strong in Scotland in the 19th century which resulted in the founding of local antiquarian societies. For some of our burghs the work of these pioneers provides us with some quite striking records of archaeological discoveries during drainage and building works. The members of Perth Literary and Antiquarian Society, for example, took it upon themselves to record such discoveries in the town. Local antiquarian Robert Scott Fittis records that a solicitor, William Ross, presented three papers to the society detailing his discoveries. William Ross tackled a question still asked to this day, 'Can you explain how the remains of the old town are so low, being close on the level of the Tay, if not in some cases below it?' and answered it by suggesting that this is due to the continuous rise in the level of the gravelly river bed. He qualified this further by pointing out that, 'the tops of the gateways in the old walls of the town are seen only a few feet above the level of the lade in Mill Street'. At the time that Ross wrote this, the Town Lade was still open right the way around the town and such evidence would have been readily visible; these days, the lade is culverted under the modern streets and such evidence of depth of deposit is only retrieved through excavation.

Perth Museum holds the records of another early recorder of Perth's archaeology, Burgh Surveyor Thomas McLaren. His section drawings of drainage works around St John's church in 1921 are probably the earliest urban medieval record drawings in Scotland.

Urban Archaeology

Urban archaeology can often provide the most information and in some ways the most striking finds of any sort of excavation. This is because many medieval towns are situated on sites where continuous occupation can often result in archaeological deposits up to 3 or 4 metres deep. The burghs of Perth and North Berwick and parts of the Old Town of Edinburgh probably represent the best Scottish examples of such survival. These deep deposits are often waterlogged and produce what are described as 'anaerobic' deposits, in effect conditions where the process of decay of organic material like leather or wood is either very slow or does not happen at all. This is why the archaeological deposits of Perth are so rich and contain artefacts and materials that do not survive elsewhere. This can often mean that artefacts are found that it is difficult to find parallels for from other burghs.

Whilst this offers the opportunity to be able to reconstruct an accurate picture of lifestyle and living conditions of up to 700 or 800 years ago, it comes at a very high financial cost. All the excavations mentioned in this book took place as the result of modern development projects, a side of archaeology that since the 1970s has been known as 'Rescue' because the material is being excavated and examined before it is destroyed by the new development. It is now the norm for such projects to be funded by the developer and in an urban context this can be so expensive that a redesign of the proposed foundations is often the preferred option thus preserving the deposits *in situ* for future archaeologists.

Medieval deposits survive better in some of Scotland's burghs than in others. Important centres such as Elgin, Forres and Dunfermline often prove to have no archaeology surviving on their street frontages. All three of these burghs are built on ridges, and their High

Reconstructions of Trench Section in Perth
Showing archaeological deposits *(left)* surviving below cellar floor and *(right)* in process of destruction.
SUAT LTD

Streets run along the top. Every phase of urban renewal scrapes the archaeology off to the natural subsoil. Downhill from the ridge, archaeological deposits will survive, often to some depth, but the important link to the buildings on the frontage will have gone. One of the major tasks facing the modern urban archaeologist is to attempt to predict where the deposits will survive and to react to development pressures accordingly.

(above)
Excavations at Meal Vennel, Perth, 1983
General view.
SUAT LTD

Multiple Clay Floors
Revealed in the side of a sewer trench in Scott Street, Perth.
SUAT LTD

Dating

The dating of medieval archaeology is based on a combination of the information provided by pottery and other excavated finds. Some types of pottery can be dated by relating them to finds elsewhere, but there are often problems when the only pottery recovered is of local production for which there is still not a usable chronology. Radiocarbon dating is not as useful for archaeology of the medieval period, because the potential error can often span a couple of centuries. Perhaps the most usable dating technique is dendrochronology – tree ring dating; a valuable database of samples is now in existence. However, to employ this dating technique you need to recover substantial pieces of timber – this is rare. As with much of our information for medieval Scotland, it is the deposits of burghs such as Perth and Aberdeen that are able to supply such samples.

Medieval Pottery
From a typical urban site in Perth.
SUAT LTD

Before the Burghs

There were no Roman towns in Scotland and the Picts are not known to have had any urban tradition: when, how and why did this process start? What sources of information are there? It was in 1072 that William the Conqueror set foot in Scotland for the only time, in Perthshire at the ancient round tower of Abernethy. He was met by Malcolm III, king of Scots, who 'made peace ... and gave hostages and was his man'. This meeting of the two kings ensured that there was never a Norman invasion of Scotland. We therefore have no Domesday Book for Scotland and our understanding of the country in the 11th and early 12th centuries is therefore not as good as England.

It is very likely that when many of the burghs were being given their foundation status, some sort of settlement already existed on the site. Such pre-burgal evidence from archaeological excavation is still quite limited, but a tantalising glimpse from Perth was the discovery of a ditch lined with wattle (tree branches woven together) which has been carbon dated to AD 990–1040. This feature may be part of an enclosure around an earlier version of St John's church and seems to indicate settlement at Perth at least 100 years earlier than its foundation as a burgh in the 12th century.

Early Christian Cemetery
Kirkhill, St Andrews, under excavation in 1980.
SUAT LTD

Another Scottish burgh with evidence of its pre-burgal origins is St Andrews in Fife. Nowadays much better known as a mecca for golfers, St Andrews originated as an early religious centre that was located on the headland at Kirkhill. Excavations in 1980 located part of a substantial cemetery which included bodies buried in stone boxes known as long cists, that have been dated from the 6th to 8th centuries AD. There almost certainly would have been a settlement associated with this early religious centre, although this has yet to be located. It seems likely that early religious settlements may have formed the nucleus of what were later to be founded as burghs.

What is a Burgh?

The use of the term 'burgh' to refer to a Scottish medieval town relates back to the concept of 'burgage', a system of ownership of land in a town. In England the term 'borough' originates from the same source.

There were five different types of burghs whose status depended on who was the driving force behind the settlement's creation. In order of status, these were royal burghs (under the control of the king), baronial burghs (under the control of a baron), ecclesiastical burghs (under the control of the church), burghs of regality, burghs dependant on abbeys, and free burghs. Essentially, the main difference in these types was that the non-royal burghs enjoyed restricted privileges, Baronial burghs, for example, were not able to undertake foreign trade and were only able to buy and sell within the confines of the burgh, not in the surrounding countryside which fell within the liberty of some royal burgh. By the 17th century, this monopoly was being challenged and in 1672, an Act of Parliament gave baronial burghs the same rights of overseas trade as the royal burghs.

The Arrival of the Burghs

**Bishop Robert
and Mainard the Fleming**

Checking progress on the laying-out of
properties on South Street, St Andrews,
in the early 12th century.
CHRISTINA UNWIN

'You who were formerly a beggar among all other countries used to inflict
famine on your inhabitants from your harsh soil; now softer and more fertile
than the others, you have relieved the poverty of neighbouring regions from
your abundance. King David adorned you with castles and cities, he raised
you up with lofty towers, he enriched your ports with foreign merchandise,
and added the riches of other kingdoms for your delight.'
Scotichronicon, Walter Bower, 1440s

It is with the succession of King David I to the
Scottish throne that the first Scottish burghs
appear. Many of David's burghs survive as
major towns today such as Perth, Aberdeen,
Stirling, Inverness, Edinburgh, Glasgow and
Dunfermline. Some did not fare as well,
however. One of the earliest Scottish burghs at
Roxburgh (by Kelso) has been deserted since
at least the late 15th century, and other deserted
burghs include Spynie (near Elgin), Cullen
(south of the modern town) and Rattray
(Aberdeenshire).

The whole concept of town planning is one
that David I seems to have learned from the
Normans and the distinctive gridded pattern of
such town plans survives in the modern town
plans of Perth and Elgin, although modern
development is beginning to blur the picture. It
is clear from the documentary record that many
of these new towns were being laid out by
foreigners, particularly from the Low
Countries. Mainard the Fleming, for example,
is on record as marking out the earliest streets
in St Andrews in the 12th century. Many 19th-
century antiquarians thought that such regular
street plans must indicate a Roman origin for
many of the Scottish burghs. This was not the
case, however, since the Roman invasion of
Scotland was essentially a military one and they
did not found any towns.

Daily Life

Although documents do survive that provide evidence for the medieval period in Scotland, most of them concern the Crown and religious matters. The most informative way of discovering what it was like to live and work in medieval Scotland is through the results of archaeological excavation. The excellent conditions for preservation in towns such as Perth, Aberdeen and parts of Elgin mean that clothing, footwear and wooden artefacts such as bowls and spoons survive. Such preservation gives the archaeologist the rare opportunity to reconstruct medieval life right through from the buildings and streetscape to what people were wearing and how they ate.

The most productive elements of a medieval burgh from the archaeologist's point of view are the town middens. In the medieval period there does not seem to have been an organised rubbish collection system, although by the 16th century there are references in burgh guildry books to 'pynnouris' or shore porters, who were paid to remove rubbish. The result was that domestic rubbish was disposed of by being spread out in the backlands of the burgage plots or even out into the street. There is documentary evidence from Perth which indicates that this build-up of rubbish was starting to cause problems by the 15th century, particularly where it was building up along the access road at the foot of the town defences: the burgh eventually passed a law to prevent this from happening.

Jet Chess Piece
From Meal Vennel excavation, Perth, dating to the 15th century.
SUAT LTD

Fragment of Textile Clothing
From a water pipe trench in Perth.

Stave-built Vessel
SUAT LTD

Complete Leather Shoe
From Perth High Street excavations.
SUAT LTD

Turned Wooden Bowl
From Kirk Close excavations, Perth, dating to the 14th or 15th century.
SUAT LTD

Decorated Leather Knife Scabbard
From excavations in Perth.
SUAT LTD

0   10 centimetres

The deep middens of Perth contain preserved textiles, silk, leather and wood that tell what clothing and footwear people were wearing. The most commonly found textile is a very coarse hand-woven fabric that was presumably very good at keeping out the cold. Finer types of clothing are best represented by the very ornate silk headscarf from Perth High Street. The best parallel for this headscarf comes from royal graves in Spain dated to the 14th century. Other fragments of silk embroidered with bird designs were recovered from the Kirk Close excavation in Perth.

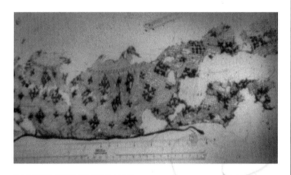

Spanish Silk Head Scarf
From Perth High Street excavations, dating to 12th or 13th centuries.
SUAT LTD

There is limited evidence for domestic sanitation – a small shed containing an earth toilet was found attached to the back of a medieval building fronting the High Street at Kirk Close, so by implication such facilities may have been very common in the medieval burgh. Locally-gathered moss seems to have been used as the equivalent of modern toilet paper. We presume that the water was provided by communal wells, although the town's lade may have been clean enough also to provide water.

In its medieval heyday Perth appears to have become a very crowded place, and pressure on the available High Street frontage seems to have been intense; this is best illustrated by the results of excavations at the House of Fraser site in the early 1980s, where a vennel (or alley) between two properties on the street frontage was turned into a very small booth by roofing over the gap between the two buildings. The enterprising occupant then appeared to be in the business of selling hot food, as there is a small hearth with an associated wattle-built animal pen perhaps for chickens. In contrast, there is evidence from excavations in Perth that in some periods, possibly as early as the mid-13th century, some of the street frontages are derelict and are only occupied by pits either for rubbish or the quarrying of sand; later examples of such bad times for the burgh economy may reflect the effect of Wars of Independence of the 14th century.

The most distinctive feature of the plans of Scotland's medieval burghs are the backlands. These reflect the way land was divided when the burghs were founded – an extent on the street frontage where the first buildings were built, and a long strip of land stretching back to the next boundary, often the limit of the burgh. In burghs such as Perth, St Andrews and Aberdeen the boundaries of many of these plots of land have remained unchanged throughout the centuries, although many have now disappeared as a result of modern development. The owners of the properties would often conduct their trade here, and it is from these backland properties that much of the archaeological evidence for the different industries of the burgh is recovered (see Trade and Industry page 20). From the surviving documentary evidence in the Rental Books of the King James VI Hospital in Perth we can see that these backlands are often further subdivided into 'forelands' and 'innerlands' and often have various owners. By careful study it is possible to construct an accurate jigsaw of how the different parts of the burgh would have looked at various periods in the late medieval and post-medieval periods.

Social Organisation

The most striking social change that took place following the foundation of the burghs was the creation of a sense of community amongst their inhabitants. This consensus was vital to ensure that important factors such as trade and industry would prosper. To qualify for burgess-ship and all the privileges that came with it, a serf had to be able to prove that they had been resident in the relevant burgh for a year and a day. Most adult males would have become burgesses – women and children enjoyed privileges through their husbands and fathers but were not involved in the political life of the burgh. As the new burghs became the focus for immigrants from the surrounding countryside, the number of non-burgesses increased. Most of these incomers lacked the necessary finance to purchase the plots of land that were required for burgess-ship and would have found employment as servants or labourers for the established inhabitants. The results of excavations in Aberdeen have led the excavator to suggest that these non-burgesses may have been housed in the buildings that have been excavated in the burgh backlands that are generally of a poorer quality than those on the frontages. Interestingly, however, excavations on Mill Street in Perth have located backland buildings dating to the 14th and 15th centuries with tiled roof ridges, surely a sign of wealth?

A Typical Scottish Merchant
SUAT LTD

There is no evidence that this segment of the population was considered to be outside the community. If anything, the family-based organisation of trades and crafts fostered a close relationship between them and the burgesses. As Elizabeth Ewan points out, for many inhabitants of the burgh the attainment of burgess status was not a crucial goal anyway; they were happy to leave the political leadership that went with it to the more important members of the burgh who had the time and money to devote to it. If the interests of the group of non-burgesses were threatened, they could appeal to the burgesses for help. In 1366, for example, a group of fishermen from the burgh of Stirling were helped in their attack on the fishings of Cambuskenneth Abbey in the Forth by 23 burgesses in the town.

Mace Head
From Kirk Close excavations in Perth. Height 5.3 cm.
SUAT LTD

Climate

Flooding in the burgh of Perth is not a modern phenomenon. As early as 1209, the royal castle was washed away and in 1621 'a fearful inundation of waters' swept away the bridge over the river. At very low water the timber pile foundations of this bridge can still be seen in the riverbed running across to Stanners Island.

Occasionally, archaeological excavation can retrieve information that can be used to reconstruct the weather conditions and climate of medieval Scotland. We know from the combination of documentary sources and environmental evidence (tree-ring growth, lake sediments) that between AD 1000 and 1200 the climate was much warmer than it is today and therefore crop yields were much higher. But after *c* AD 1300 things changed for the worse, with the onset of what is known as the Little Ice Age which lasted for nearly five centuries. During this period the annual temperature seems to have dropped by at least one degree Centigrade and the prevailing winds seemed to have shifted to being more frequently from a northerly or north-easterly direction.

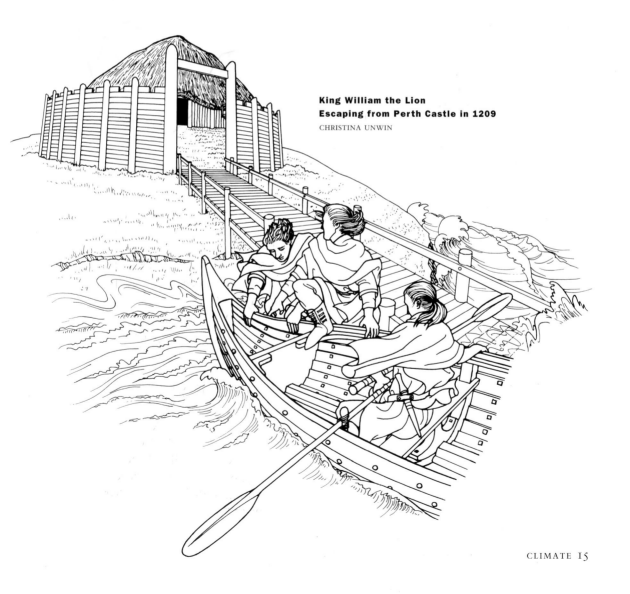

**King William the Lion
Escaping from Perth Castle in 1209**
CHRISTINA UNWIN

Several excavations on the east coast have indicated that wind-blown sand used to pose some problems. In North Berwick, Montrose and Arbroath, for example, archaeologists have recognised banded layers of sand between occupation deposits. A similar situation seems to have existed on the west coast which is why the Sandgate in Ayr is so named. Evidence for climatic variation can also be recovered, for example the bone ice skates from Perth indicate a period when the River Tay must have frozen over.

Deep Archaeological Deposits and Wind-blown Sand
High Street, North Berwick.
SUAT LTD

Bone Ice Skates
From King Edward Street excavations in Perth.
SUAT LTD

Reconstruction of Ice Skates in Use
SUAT LTD

Buildings and Townscape

The very good preservation of archaeological deposits in burghs such as Perth and Aberdeen has allowed us to suggest what the standard domestic dwellings of the medieval burgh must have looked like. Until at least the 15th or 16th century, all the buildings were built of wood – the only stone-built structures were liable to have been the church and any monastic establishments, although there is an intriguing reference to a stone house in 14th-century Perth. A standard medieval house would have had timber foundation-beams holding upright posts that supported wattle walls daubed with clay and dung. Occasionally, evidence is found for a slightly more sophisticated wall structure, such as upright planks fitted together with tongue and groove. The roofs of these medieval buildings seem to have been thatched

(above)
Wattle Wall
From Kirk Close excavation, Perth, showing daub partially removed.
SUAT LTD

(left)
Excavated Building
Postholes indicating the ground plan of a medieval timber building on Perth High Street.
SUAT LTD

Reconstruction

Of a typical medieval wooden building.

SUAT LTD

with straw or heather, although it has been argued recently that wooden shingles may also have been used – there is a single excavated example of a shingle from the Marks and Spencer's site excavations in Perth. An account of the Perth flood of 1209 refers to some of the burgesses escaping from the rising waters by going upstairs into the 'solars' of their houses, implying that some of these houses must have had at least two storeys.

The buildings would have been concentrated on the street frontage and along the sides of any vennels or closes that ran back from these major thoroughfares. Vennels seem to have been a very common feature of the burghs, and some still exist to this day, for example Horner's Vennel and Cutlog Vennel in Perth or the many closes of Edinburgh's Royal Mile. The name 'vennel' is French in origin and provides further evidence for Norman influence in the planning of the burghs.

From excavations in the east coast burghs, evidence is growing that the High Streets of these towns were often much wider than now, by up to as much as 2 or 3 metres on either side. It appears that these wide streets were the sites of the markets for the burgh, as the market square, so common in England, is a rare phenomenon in Scotland.

Very few burghs were provided with formal defences against attack; Perth was one of the few that had a substantial stone wall surrounded by a deep water-filled ditch. In most other burghs the ends of the long backlands (known as head riggs) would also have served as a boundary to the burgh. Most major Scottish burghs also possessed a royal castle although few now survive; Perth's castle was washed away in the floods of 1209 and was never rebuilt. That the king subsequently stayed at the Blackfriars monastery when visiting Perth implies that the main function of these castles was as royal lodgings and not as defensive strongholds. One of the few burgh castles that archaeologists have excavated is the one that used to stand on Ladyhill at the west end of the modern High Street in Elgin; when it was examined in 1973, evidence for at least two defensive ramparts surrounding a timber palisade was recovered. The finds include a substantial number of deer bones, which showed that hunting played an important part in the life of the occupants of the castle. Excavations at the castles of Strachan in Aberdeenshire and Peebles in the Scottish Borders have suggested that these buildings often comprised a circular timber hall surrounded by a palisade standing on an artificial mound (motte). Slezer's 18th-century view of Elgin seems to indicate a similar structure standing on Ladyhill.

Access to a harbour was important to the success of a medieval burgh; Perth, Dundee and Dumbarton were very successful as a result, whereas burghs like Elgin had to rely on a harbour some 5 miles away at Spynie. Although St Andrews did have a harbour, it could not accommodate very large ships and therefore did not attract very much foreign trade.

Trade and Industry

Many of the burghs were hives of commercial activity and different parts of town were used by different trades, as may be reflected by some of the street and vennel names that survive, Skinnergate and Horner's Vennel in Perth being good examples. Thirteenth-century documents give us an idea of the number and types of trades or professions that existed in Scotland's burghs. People's names included their trade, *Willelmus galeator* (helmet maker) and *Robertus faber* (smith). Such trade names were associated with a range of industrial processes involving cloth or clothing, metalwork and leatherwork. It is out of this wide range of professions that the Guildry Incorporation developed, an organisation that still exists today in many Scottish towns. By 1400, at least 13 burghs are on record as having guilds; unfortunately, no earlier records of these important organisations survive which makes it difficult to understand their function and composition. In Perth, the Guilds of Glovers and Hammermen (metalworkers) claim that their origins go back to the time of William the Lion (12th/13th centuries). The presence of guilds in most of the burghs involved in overseas trade suggests that they had a monopoly over trade in certain goods such as cloth and hides.

It is interesting to identify which industries were not members of the Guildry as this may imply that they were not based within the burgh limits – the pottery industry for example. The kiln sites which produced large quantities of pottery do not seem to have been located

Collapsed Wattle
Built cover for an industrial feature, Kirk Street excavation, Perth.
SUAT LTD

within the burgh limits, although from the excavations at Marks and Spencer's on Perth's High Street alone there are *c* 50,000 sherds of pottery. The kilns would, of course, have been an enormous fire hazard to a town almost exclusively built of timber. Until the post-medieval period, basic cooking equipment was made of ceramic material, although plates and bowls were exclusively made from wood. Whereas broken wooden implements could be burnt, pottery is virtually indestructible and so is a common find from excavations. In the case of Perth there are at least three possible sites for pottery kilns: at Claypots, Potterhill and Kinnoull. However, no evidence for anything relating to such an industry has been found at any of these sites. It is possible that the kilns may have been further afield, although the first piece of kiln furniture from medieval Perth was found from the excavations on the site of the new Council Headquarters at the former Pullar's works just to the north of the medieval burgh. It seems likely that a whole series of small kiln sites situated in rural settlements may have been supplying the major burghs, since in many cases this is where the resources, a clay fuel and water supply, are located anyway

At the time of writing, the products of a native pottery industry have been identified, but very few kiln sites have either been located or excavated. From at least the 12th century Scottish White Gritty ware was being produced, with suggested production centres in the Borders, Lothian and Fife. There is a strong possibility that the technology for producing this well-fired pottery may have been brought to Scotland by some of the monastic orders, particularly those orders whose mother houses were in Yorkshire.

Until the 13th century, most pottery in the burghs had been imported from England and the Low Countries. From several sites in Perth only imported pottery was found in the early layers and it is possible that the prevalence of these imported wares reflects the nationality of a large number of the burgh's inhabitants. From the early 13th century, a type of pottery called East Coast Redware came into use; it has been found in excavations from Stirling to Dornoch. A local Redware fabric is also beginning to be found on the west coast at sites in Dumfries and Galloway and in parts of Strathclyde. In 13th- and 14th-century Scotland, the very well made products of the Yorkshire kilns became the dominant type and had an enormous effect on the style and technique of the local potters. The Yorkshire kilns were producing distinctively lustrous green glazed vessels, often decorated with figures on horseback riding around the outside – for example the so-called 'knight jug' and tableware such as the aquamanile which was designed to hold water for washing the hands. Recent excavations at the site of the new Scottish Parliament in the burgh of Canongate (now in Edinburgh) have recovered an important group of 16th- and 17th-century pottery, including sherds from high-quality vessels from northern Germany and France and olive jars from Seville in Spain. Such pottery is not often recovered in Scotland, as deposits of this period have often been destroyed by the extensive 18th- and 19th-century rebuilding. The same assemblage also contains a piece of ceramic stove-tile, which possibly originated in the Baltic. Fragments of these stoves are very rare finds indeed and are evidence for a type of central heating that was popular among elite society in Britain in the sixteenth century.

The nature and extent of trade in medieval Scotland is a matter of considerable debate. The lack of surviving medieval port books makes it very difficult to prove conclusively that pottery

Medieval stone-built corn-dryer
Forth Street Lane, North Berwick.
SUAT LTD

was being traded in its own right rather than as containers for other goods such as wine and honey. However, the use of cooking pots imported from the Low Countries or Scandinavia in the early centuries of the burgh of Perth suggests that these vessels were being bought for that very purpose.

The surviving customs records indicate the export to the Low Countries and Flanders of wool from Scotland, much of which may well have been coming from the major monastic estates of the Borders. Following the end of the war between the Hanseatic League and the kingdoms of Denmark and Norway in 1370, the reopening of the Sound of Skagerrack to shipping provided direct contact between Scotland and the Baltic. Interestingly, a Hanseatic decree of this date specifically stated that Scotsmen, Englishmen and Welshmen were not permitted to salt herring at the fairs in the Baltic region. It is difficult to work out just how extensive the use of this trade route was anyway, although by 1497 the Sound Toll Register lists 21 Scots ships from Dundee, Leith, Aberdeen, St Andrews and one unknown port. Recent important work on the tree-ring dating of timbers from Stirling Castle seems to indicate that timber from the Baltic was certainly being imported into Scotland in the 15th and 16th centuries.

Animal skins, hides, cheap cloth and salt were all exported from Scotland. In the later Middle Ages there was a large-scale emigration of Scots to northern Europe; some of these were students heading for universities in Germany, France and the countries surrounding the Baltic, but many were merchants who settled in coastal ports such as Danzig. There are also tantalising pieces of evidence which may suggest that there were even earlier contacts between the Baltic States and Scotland, for example a type of imported pottery found in early levels in Perth has been identified as possibly originating in Jutland. Such possible early contacts are still the subject of ongoing research.

Archaeological excavation has now recovered evidence for the metalworking industries of the burgh of Perth as evidenced by the smelting and working of iron for the

Corn-dryer
Corn-dryer in property fronting onto Bonnygate, Cupar.
SUAT LTD

manufacture of knives, horseshoes and even barrel padlocks at the Meal Vennel. Important evidence for the source of the raw material for this industry has also been recovered, with the suggestion that 'bog iron' was probably the most commonly used and that this would have been available to both urban and rural smiths alike. Excavations at King Edward Street in Perth located a small workshop on the High Street frontage, which contained a small hearth and possible evidence for the working of either gold or silver. Leather-working was also a staple industry in the Scottish medieval burgh, producing shoes, belts, scabbards and perhaps pieces of clothing. The area around the Skinnergate in Perth was certainly the focus of this industry and many hundreds of pieces of leather have been recovered from excavations in the burgh. Slight traces of horn-working have also been recovered with rubbish pits containing discarded animal horns from which the cores have been removed being discovered. So far little detailed information for the actual processes and natures of the workshops for both these industries has been recovered.

Merchant's Seal
From Meal Vennel excavation, Perth.
SUAT LTD

Green Man Knife Handle
From Perth High Street excavation.
PERTH MUSEUM AND ART GALLERY, PERTH, SCOTLAND

(left)
Blacksmith's Hearth and Anvil Base
Meal Vennel excavation, Perth.
SUAT LTD

Religion

It seems fair to say that religion played a much greater part in people's lives in the medieval period than it does today. This probably reflects the uncertainty of people's existence and the fact that, unlike today, they would have known very little about the rest of the world and its cultures. Religion therefore offered a common experience that people could relate to. The religious orders were able to exploit this and a thriving medieval burgh offered a substantial source of revenue. These institutions were often founded by the king or a local abbey who had identified both the need for such a monastic presence and the opportunity for the relevant order to become landowners.

Most Scottish medieval burghs possessed a parish church at their core, and many of the more important burghs also possessed at least one friary, usually built beyond the burgh limits where land was much cheaper. Like many thriving medieval burghs, Perth became a focal point for the foundation of religious houses. By the mid-15th century Perth possessed four, all of them beyond the burgh limits. The earliest foundation was that of the Dominicans or Blackfriars in 1231. This friary lay on the north side of the burgh to the east of Kinnoull Street at its junction with Carpenter Street, as recently confirmed by excavation. Following the destruction of the castle by the flood of 1209, the Dominican friary seems to have become the

Friary Church Under Construction
Based on excavated evidence from the Carmelite friaries of Perth, Aberdeen and Linlithgow.
ABERDEEN MUSEUM AND ART GALLERY, ABERDEEN, SCOTLAND

Window Glass
Fragment of 13th-century painted glass from the excavation of the Carmelite church, Perth.
SUAT LTD

Carmelite Church
North Queensferry.
SUAT LTD

favoured lodging of Scottish kings when they were visiting the burgh. Indeed, it was in the Blackfriars monastery that James I was murdered in 1437.

The second foundation was that of the Carmelite friary of Tullilum in 1262. This friary lay to the west of Perth on the southern side of the Longcauseway (now Jeanfield Road). Why it is located so far away from the burgh limits is still not understood, although there is a chance that a church already existed on the site that was then granted to the Carmelites. The eastern end of the friary complex was excavated in advance of redevelopment in 1982 and some idea of the layout of the complex and the nature of the buildings was gained. The most interesting find from Whitefriars was the friary seal matrix. This object would have been used to sign letters to the pope in Rome and other important people. It is made of copper alloy and depicts the Virgin Mary breastfeeding the baby Jesus above a friar kneeling in adoration. Around the outside of the seal is inscribed *S' Prioris Fratrum Carmel de Pert* – The seal of the prior and brethren of the Carmelites of Perth. This seal is the first to be found from an excavation of a friary in Scotland. Although others

Seal Matrix
Official seal matrix of the Perth Carmelite friary, dating to the 13th century.
SUAT LTD

exist, they are in private antiquarian collections and their precise findspots are unknown.

Perth's other two religious houses were the Franciscan and Carthusian friaries. The Franciscan or Greyfriars monastery was founded in 1460 and lay to the south-east of the burgh in the area now occupied by Greyfriars cemetery. The Carthusian friary was founded in 1429 and lay to the south-west of the burgh close to the site of King James VI hospital. Known as the Vale of Virtue, it was the only Carthusian house in Scotland which must reflect the importance of Perth at that time. James I and his consort, Joan of Beaufort, were both buried there. Both Franciscan and Carthusian friaries remain archaeologically unexplored at the time of writing. Two other Carmelite friaries at Linlithgow and Aberdeen and a Franciscan friary at Jedburgh have also been excavated. Both the Linlithgow and Jedburgh friary excavations produced important information about the layout of these monastic complexes

The Reformation of 1559 played a major part in the disappearance of many of these religious institutions although the concept of wholesale mob destruction of the buildings is probably outdated. It seems much more likely that the roofs of the buildings were removed, the occupants ejected, and the stonework then gradually removed for reuse elsewhere.

The Blackfriars Brothpot Incident

Reconstruction of the Blackfriars brothpot incident, 16th-century Perth.
SUAT LTD

Church and Graveyard

Holy Trinity Parish Church, St Andrews
Dating to 1415.
SUAT LTD

Many medieval parish churches are still in use today and there have been very few excavations of their sites. It is quite striking how the locations of many of the burgh graveyards have been forgotten and that the only time that people appreciate the fact that some of the former inhabitants of the burgh are buried under their feet is when graveyards are exposed by modern development such as water and sewer-pipe renewal. The burgh graveyard of Perth, for example, used to lie all around the church of St John before it was moved to Greyfriars in 1580. It now lies under St John's Street and St John's Place. A few medieval parish churches such as St Christopher's, Cupar, and St John's, Ayr, for example, were not situated inside the burghs and may indicate important early religious foci that continued in use. Holy Trinity, the parish church of St Andrews, used to lie inside the precinct of the Augustinian abbey and cathedral until 1415 when it was moved to its modern site in South Street. Occasionally tantalising clues to the early origins of some of these sites are found. During 19th-century roadworks in Elgin, a Pictish cross-slab was found directly outside St Giles' Church. Is it possible that this stone, known as the Elgin pillar, indicates a much earlier ecclesiastical settlement in the area?

Burials
Skeletons in the parish church graveyard now under Logies Lane, St Andrews.
SUAT LTD

Health and Welfare

Without full-scale excavation of a burgh graveyard it is difficult to get an accurate picture of the health and welfare of our medieval ancestors. Our knowledge of the health and welfare therefore of the occupants of our medieval burghs is biased towards the information that has been recovered from the excavations at several monastic houses. The average lifespan in medieval times has been estimated to be 35 years for males and 31 years for females. In the small sample from Perth Blackfriars, at least eight individuals approached or achieved this age. No individual showed evidence of age changes characteristic of what we would consider late middle or old age. Indeed, the oldest individual was considered to be no more than 40 years old. This raises the question of how representative this Perth sample is of the general population of the medieval burgh. If the friary had a role in caring for the sick, it may be that this is the segment of the population represented here. However, the absence of the very old and the very young may argue against this case. The relative absence of evidence of chronic illness may indicate that the role of the friary may have been related to the care of the acutely ill, possibly those suffering from infections. One body found during the Perth excavation may have been accidentally buried alive – it was found lying face down with its elbows raised as if it was trying to escape from the grave. In early modern times, such medical errors led to many coffins being provided with bell pulls to enable occupants to inform the outside world that they were still alive.

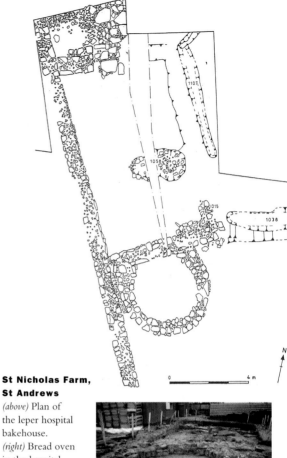

St Nicholas Farm, St Andrews
(above) Plan of the leper hospital bakehouse.
(right) Bread oven in the hospital bakehouse.
SUAT LTD

Leprosy is a disease that was widespread in Scotland from at least the 12th century. It is generally assumed that the disease reached Britain with the Crusaders returning from the Levant. By the 15th century all the major east coast burghs possessed a leper hospital. Leprosy appears to have lasted in Scotland until the 1700s, when it gradually disappeared, the southern areas becoming free of it before the north. By the 16th century every major Scottish burgh possessed a leper house and although not all the inhabitants of these hospitals may have had the disease, these institutions performed an important function in everyday life in the medieval town. The Scottish leper hospital is still poorly understood and only one, just outside St Andrews, has been excavated in recent years.

Tiled floor
Trinitarian friary, Dunbar.
SUAT LTD

Smaller hospitals or hostels also existed in the Middle Ages specifically to aid pilgrims who were *en route* to a holy shrine. One such 13th-century foundation existed at Scotlandwell on the north side of Loch Leven. This establishment lay on the western pilgrim route to St Andrews and was administered by the Trinitarians or Redfriars who only had eight houses in Scotland.

One of these, at Dunbar, was the site of some small-scale excavations in the 1980s, which revealed that the dovecot that stands at Friarscroft is actually the reused tower of the friary church. The church building contained remains of a green and yellow chequered tiled floor which was located on the east side of this structure. A major hospital also existed at Soutra in the Scottish Borders beside the main southern routeway into Scotland (formerly the Roman road known as Ermine Street). There has been some small-scale excavation at this site which has concentrated on retrieving as much information as possible about medical practices such as blood letting. In many parts of Scotland you will still find place-names that contain the word 'Spittal' but this is more likely to indicate lands that were owned by hospitals rather than the location of actual hospital sites.

Plaque
Indicating the site of St Leonard's Hospital, Perth.
SUAT LTD

The plague

The worst epidemic in European history, the Black Death (bubonic plague), entered southern England in summer 1348 through the port of Melcombe Regis (now Weymouth). This disease was spread widely throughout the country by rats. In 1349 the plague had crossed the border with the Scots army who appear to have caught it from the English army. From the available documentary evidence it would appear that, as now, the poor were more affected than the rich due to their living conditions and poor nutritional diet. Andrew of Wyntoun, a 14th-century Scottish chronicler, wrote:

> it was sayd, off lywand (living) men
> The thyrd part if dystroyid then.

And such devastation of the population may not have been an exaggeration, although it is very difficult to identify the same level of desertion of settlement in Scotland as happened in England.

Epidemics returned in the 14th and 15th centuries but were of much smaller scale. However, by the 16th century the plague and typhus were endemic and suspicion arose that the disease was being spread by contact with goods and baggage, and cloth and clothes legislation slowly appeared to deal with it. In 16th-century Leith for example, the king forbade the 'packing and peeling' of goods in Leith and the Canongate and the selling of foreign goods in the port. There has been very little archaeological evidence recovered so far from all the excavations in the Scottish burghs that can be directly linked with the various plague outbreaks; indeed, animal bone from either brown or black rats is non-existent.

Burgh Case Studies

The South and the Borders

Our knowledge of the medieval burghs of south-west Scotland is still very limited due to the lack of work that has taken place.

PEEBLES

Excavations have taken place at two sites in Peebles at Cuddyside and Bridgegate. Neither found any trace of the late 16th-century town wall erected around the burgh, but they did uncover important information on the origins of settlement there. The results obtained from the excavations call for a reappraisal of the supposed date of the settlement of the peninsular ridge between the Tweed and Eddleston Water. Traditionally, settlement is not supposed to have occurred until the 15th century. However, at both sites, occupation, in the form of stone structures, can be dated to the 14th century at the latest, with probable earlier dumping of domestic refuse in the 12th and 13th centuries. This dumping was presumably carried out from settlement elsewhere on the ridge, rather than from Old Town across the Eddleston. It seems possible, if not probable, that settlement on the ridge dates from the foundation of the royal castle on Castle Hill under David I (1124–53). Excavations on this

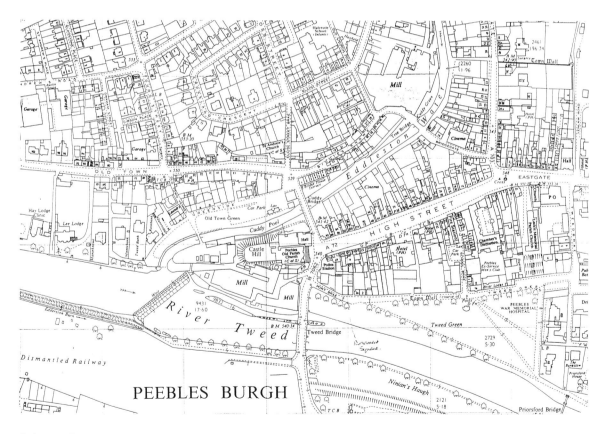

Ordnance Survey Map of Peebles
ORDNANCE SURVEY

site in 1978 recovered the ground plan of the castle, which seemed to comprise a circular timber keep.

Presumably, the early settlement began close to the castle, expanding eastwards along the ridge to reach both sites by the 14th century. The street of Bridgegate was apparently laid out in the 13th or 14th century when the excavation site was divided into three properties aligned on the street, two of which had stone buildings erected on them. One of these buildings seems to have been a merchant's house of two storeys.

Alternatively, Bridgegate may have been the initial focus of settlement on the east side of the Eddleston, providing the access route from the east into Old Town, where a pilgrimage centre had been established at the Cross Kirk in 1261, and the location of the tolbooth in it suggests that this street was originally more important than High Street. The Cuddyside excavations raise the possibility that the structures there may have been originally situated in backlands of properties aligned on Bridgegate, rather than on High Street. However, the Bridgegate excavations revealed that, on the north side of the street, two plots extended back only some 14 metres from the street frontage with no evidence that they had been curtailed in a subsequent laying out of Northgate, while the Cuddyside structures were some 25 metres from the Bridgegate frontage. It seems more likely that the Cuddyside structures were in backlands of a property aligned on High Street.

In 1466, the burgh was divided into five areas, four of which were named streets on the east side of the Eddleston Water – High Street, Crossgate, Northgate and Bridgegate – while the supposed original centre of the burgh on the west side of the Eddleston was merely an unnamed street 'beyond the Watter'. It is surely evident that the supposed 'new' settlement must have been both long established and the main centre of population of the burgh for a considerable time before.

It is noteworthy that all eight medieval buildings excavated so far in Peebles have been stone-built. While it is possible that any trace of earlier timber structures may have been removed during the construction of these stone structures, it is equally possible that stone construction was a preferred option from the beginning, due either to the availability of stone instead of timber for building or to the probability of flooding from the nearby Eddleston Water.

Of the structures found in Bridgegate, the tolbooth was the most important, being the civic centre of the burgh. Peebles tolbooth is the only medieval tolbooth site in Scotland to have been excavated. (With the exception of Crail, where a portion of the tolbooth may date from 1517, the earliest standing tolbooths date from the second half of the 16th century.) The ground plan comprised two rooms, covering an area at least 12 metres long by 5 metres wide, internally. Access to the upper floor(s) which contained the council chamber and other public offices would have been by an external stair (no trace of which was found). It was common for the basements or cellars of tolbooths to be rented out for storage or shops, but it is curious that in the mid-16th century the cellar or basement at Peebles was being used for such a noxious industry as tanning. No evidence for a steeple attached to the tolbooth (a common feature on other examples) was found.

The layout of the ground floor of the tolbooth resembles that of the other excavated buildings, a stone structure of the 14th century which remained in use until the early 20th century. This structure probably began as a merchant's house of two storeys, with two rooms, possibly workshops, on the ground floor divided by a cross-passage, and living accommodation on the upper floor serviced by an external garderobe (latrine) pit. To have survived for such a long time, despite the vicissitudes of English raids and structural alterations, the building must have been of good construction (or had a succession of impoverished owners).

Medieval Stone Building
Cuddyside excavations in Peebles.
SUAT LTD

Only small quantities of imported medieval pottery have been found at Peebles: less than 1 per cent at Bridgegate, Peebles, and none at Cuddyside. At Bridgegate, the presence of two sherds of Low Countries Greyware hint that occupation on the south and east side of the Eddleston Water could also have begun as early as the 12th century. This may reflect the situation in most Scottish medieval burghs that were at some distance from major ports.

The work so far in Peebles highlights the contrast that is evident in the pastoral economy of the Borders burghs in comparison to that of other burghs in northern and eastern Scotland. Excavations in the northern and eastern burghs have shown that cattle were the mainstay of their local economies, whereas sheep were predominant in both the medieval and post-medieval periods at Bridgegate, Peebles. This difference between the pastoral economy in the Borders and that elsewhere in Scotland is also apparent in animal bone excavated from Eyemouth and Jedburgh friary. Such a contrast between the Borders and northern and eastern Scotland is hardly surprising given the documentary evidence for the sheep farming practised by the religious houses of Melrose, Kelso and Coldingham and by the Crown in the Borders.

Otherwise, the evidence from animal bones is consistent with that from excavations in other burghs. Pigs played little part as a source of food, nor did deer. That bones of mature sheep and cattle were common suggests that they were reared for wool and milk respectively and that good animal husbandry was practised (winter fodder must also have been in good supply). Butchery marks on bones confirm that meat cleavers rather than saws were used to disjoint carcasses, even into the modern period.

Apart from a late 16th-century corn-drying kiln from a site in Kelso and the tanning pits in the basement of the tolbooth of Peebles, no structural evidence of industrial activity has been found in the excavations at Kelso or Peebles. Analysis of grain from the kiln revealed that barley, wheat and wild oats were being dried; also found were weeds consistent with crop growing and wasteland. Metalworking was evident in the form of slag and lead alloy waste. A local pottery industry is evident in both the medieval and post-medieval periods at Kelso, although no kiln sites are known for the medieval period. The Decorated Slipwares of the post-medieval period show strong Dutch and German influences on the local industry. Textile working would have been a domestic activity, as evident from the personal equipment recovered from the excavations, such as pins, needles and thimbles.

The results of the excavations have shown that in both Kelso and Peebles much archaeological information can be retrieved on their medieval and post-medieval origins and growth, even in areas previously thought to have little significance in the burghs. The results of the excavations have shown that in both Kelso and Peebles much archaeological information can be retrieved on their medieval and post-medieval origins and growth, even in areas previously thought to have little significance in the burghs.

The West Coast

Archaeological work in the medieval burghs of Scotland's west coast has been on a much smaller scale than on the east coast. However, work in Ayr (detailed below) and Dumbarton has indicated that there are interesting differences in the external influences on the different sides of the country. Although work in Dumbarton has been very limited, it is clear from recent excavations that deep archaeological deposits survive on the north side of the High Street. Fairly intensive industrial activity identified in these excavations may relate to the refurbishment of the Scottish fleet in the late 15th and early 16th centuries at a time when Dumbarton had been chosen as the shipbuilding and outfitting base for the

Scottish navy. The pottery recovered from late medieval and early post-medieval levels in Dumbarton has added to our knowledge of the ceramics of this later period and has provided the first known findspots in Scotland of both Donyatt Ware from Somerset and Italian tin-glazed Polychrome Ware. The assemblage, which complements those recovered from other west coast burghs such as Ayr, Paisley and Glasgow, indicates trading links and inland networks markedly different from those of the east coast burghs; the west coast burghs engaged in trade with France, Germany, Spain, Italy and the west coast of England, the east coast burghs with the Low Countries and northern England.

AYR

Ayr possesses the earliest surviving charter of erection of any royal burgh in Scotland. The location of the burgh is largely due to the excellent natural harbour at the mouth of the River Ayr. The original burgh grew up in the shadow of William the Lion's castle, which was founded in 1197. There appears to have been a settlement or at least a castle at Ayr prior to its foundation as a royal burgh in the early 13th century. It is likely that this pre-charter settlement was located along the Sandgate but that the problems of inundations of wind-blown sand forced a major reorientation, with the High Street becoming the focus of the new

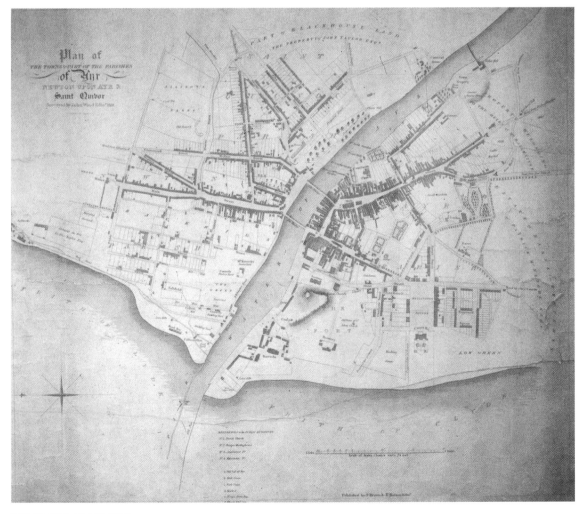

Wood's Map of Ayr 1818

royal burgh. This seems to be the reason why many important burgh buildings such as tolbooths and market crosses are duplicated. This gives the medieval burgh an L-shaped layout with Sandgate forming the foot.

However, the earliest pottery from excavations in Ayr, dating to the 12th century, came from a backland site at 51 High Street, virtually at the heart of the medieval burgh, near where the second tolbooth and market cross were situated. In addition, pottery, quantities of medieval window glass and disturbed human bone fragments, dating to the late 12th and 13th centuries, were recovered from the earliest deposits excavated beside the site of the Franciscan friary at 102–4 High Street. The window glass may have come from an otherwise unrecorded early church or chapel. All these finds suggest that the pre-burghal settlement, with a church or chapel, could have been centred on High Street, near

the site of the later bridge, rather than on Sandgate.

There are, however, a number of reasons for questioning this view. From architectural fragments still surviving at St John's Tower it is clear that the parish church was not built until later, about the time of the foundation of the castle and burgh of Ayr, about 1197. Also, the Main Street of the adjacent burgh, Newton, is situated opposite Sandgate, both streets lying on the main route from Glasgow to the south-west. This implies that the ford across the river between them was the earliest major crossing point, before the construction, further upstream in the 15th century, of the present Auld Brig, which replaced another ford there. Settlement at Newton dates from at least the early 13th century, and as the bridge of Ayr (presumably timber) is first recorded about the same time, in 1236, the earliest bridge may have been at the end of Sandgate, not on the

Medieval 'Auld Brig' of Ayr
SUAT LTD

site of the Auld Brig off High Street. Moreover, the castle was sited near the fords between Sandgate and Main Street and between the harbour and Newton Green. Therefore, Sandgate was clearly the more important routeway and the more likely location of the pre-burghal settlement.

Three excavations have taken place near the western edge of the medieval burgh (marked by Fort Street) in backlands of rigs or properties fronting on Sandgate. The layout of the western side of the burgh is unusual in that the western end of the properties on the west side of Sandgate lay beyond the sites of the Boat or Sea Port and the Kirk Port. Also, the port, indicated on Tessin's plan at the end of School Vennel, lies beyond the line of both the Boat and Kirk Ports. This may mean that at some stage after these last two ports were constructed the rigs were extended and School Vennel inserted into the layout. Truncation of the rigs at the southern end of Sandgate as a result of the construction of the citadel is evident from Tessin's plan.

On the evidence of pottery recovered from the series of excavations along the west side of High Street, at least two separate stages of expansion of the burgh of Ayr can be identified. Sites at 167–9 and 187–95 High Street respectively, produced pottery and evidence of occupation from the 14th century. However, a site at 213–17 High Street, while producing a few earlier, residual sherds, does not seem to have been developed until the 16th century. The location of the Kyle Port at 183–5 High Street suggests that it marked the southern limit of the medieval burgh on High Street. Presumably the port was in existence long before it is first mentioned in a document of 1601. Expansion beyond the port was apparently gradual and intermittent before the 16th century, but did take place. In 1862, a coin hoard, comprising 135 English and Scottish coins of the 15th century, was found in the Wheatsheaf Inn, to the north of 213–17 High Street. The coins must have been concealed inside a building on the site in the 15th century.

NEWTON UPON AYR

The difference in status between the royal burgh of Ayr and the baronial burgh of Newton is reflected in the pottery recovered from the excavations in both burghs. The absence of Saintonge Polychrome Ware (production of which seems to have ceased in the early 14th century) from the Newton sites suggests that the burgh of Newton was founded after that time, late in the 14th century, over a century after Ayr itself. Different local pottery fabrics from Newton and Ayr indicate different local trade networks for each burgh. Also the presence of more imported pottery in the Ayr sites than in Newton reflects the monopoly that the royal burghs exercised over foreign trade. The presence of more Greyware – a lower status pottery type – in Newton than in Ayr may relect the poorer status of Newton from the 15th century onwards.

Traces of three or four medieval timber buildings constructed of stake-and-wattle walls based in trenches with rounded corners have been found in Ayr. These are the earliest domestic buildings to have been found, and are dated by pottery to the 14th–15th century. These buildings are surprisingly far back – some 50 metres – from the street frontage. Buildings dated to the 12th–13th century have also been found 40 metres back from the frontage in excavations at Perth High Street.

By the first half of the 14th century there were at least three stone buildings in Ayr: in Woodgate (now High Street) before 1340; and in Seagate (now Boat Vennel), and near the corner of Doongate (now Sandgate) and Woodgate in 1348. The source of stone for these buildings may have been the stone quarry in 'Quarrier Street' (*vicus lapidarii*, possibly the later Mill Vennel, now Mill Street). The earliest domestic building still standing from medieval Ayr is Loudoun Hall, a stone structure dating to the early 16th century. Lady Cathcart's House, the second oldest domestic building in Ayr, dates from the early 17th century with later additions and alterations. A stone building, constructed about 1470, stood in backlands at 68–70 High Street until it was demolished in 1972.

The medieval economy of Ayr was based on producing raw materials and processing them into manufactured goods for sale. These raw materials were of two types: organic, derived from animal husbandry, cultivation of crops, and from fishing; and mineral, based on metalworking or stone quarrying. Coal production before the 17th century was limited.

Animal husbandry involved rearing of cattle, sheep and pigs as sources of food and raw materials. Cattle were the main source of meat, followed by sheep or goats, with pigs a poor third. Horses were also being butchered, though whether for human consumption or feeding dogs is unclear. By-products of animals included hides and wool (neither of which survived in the archaeological record) and bone, horn and antler for working into objects for everyday use. Cats and dogs were skinned for their furs. Examination of animal bones indicates that butchery of animal carcasses was done with axes or cleavers rather than saws before the modern period. This fits in with similar evidence from other medieval and post-medieval urban sites in Scotland. Weaving and spinning of wool would have been largely a domestic occupation in the medieval period.

Evidence of slots dug for cultivation, that allow for a controlled mix of manure and soil, was found at some sites in Ayr and Newton, probably for vegetables. Similar features have also been located on excavations in St Andrews. The only environmental evidence from excavations in Ayr came from South Harbour Street, where seeds of oats and barley and remains of cereal were recovered from the backfill of a 15th-century midden pit. Seeds of

bramble, presumably collected rather than cultivated, and fig, an import, indicate supplements to a diet of cereals and meat. Fish also supplemented the diet. Arable weeds and wetland weeds were also found elsewhere on the site, the latter indicating the marshy nature of the nearby riverside and the sand dunes to the west of the burgh.

At the South Harbour Street site, definite remains of industrial features were revealed in the form of a furnace or kiln, constructed of clay-bonded sandstone, with associated quenching trough or water tank. These were dated to the 14th century on the basis of pottery evidence. Unfortunately, no evidence of the purpose of the kiln was found.

At St John's Tower, specialist industrial activity is indicated by a bell casting pit for making the bell of the church. Other specialist activity can be assumed for glazing the windows of the church, although no evidence for working glass on site was found. References in the burgh accounts to repairs to the church and tolbooth windows from the 16th century indicate that there were glaziers in Ayr. A necessary accompaniment to the glazing was lead working for the strips – cames – to hold the glass; a fragment of lead alloy waste may be debris from such activity.

A local pottery industry is indicated from the identification of a local fabric; indeed, it is evident that there were separate industries in Ayr and Newton. A fragment of a small bowl, encrusted with copper oxide, was found at St John's Tower. It may have been used in the pottery industry as a vessel in which copper oxides were crushed to prepare green glazes for pots or tiles.

As a royal burgh with a harbour, medieval Ayr enjoyed a monopoly over the internal and external trade within its hinterland of Kyle and Carrick. The trade links of the burgh, as evidenced from ceramic imports, were markedly different from those of east coast burghs. The latter participated in a North Sea trade network, bringing in Low Countries,

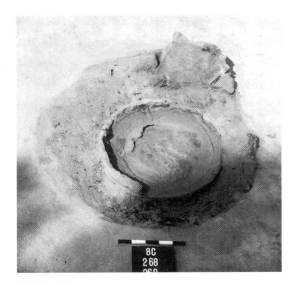

Bell Mould

From excavations at St John's Tower, Ayr.

SUAT LTD

German, French and English ceramics. Ayr, by contrast, being a west coast port, does not seem to have participated in this network. Its ceramic imports were primarily French, with little Low Countries, German and eastern English ceramics.

This contrast is hardly surprising given Ayr's geographical position: the scarcity of Yorkshire wares there is shared with Dublin, where the pattern of English ceramic imports has been shown to have been predominantly south-western and western England. Nevertheless, the general lack of English wares from Ayr is puzzling. A downturn in English ceramic imports might be expected to have occurred in the 14th century, as a result of the Wars of Independence. So, for the first century of its existence, Ayr could have enjoyed trade links bringing in English wares. Indeed, for the first decade or so of the 14th century Ayr was occupied by an English garrison. Only more archaeological research in other west coast burghs may clarify their links with England and the North Sea network.

The East Coast

Archaeological excavations in Scotland's east coast burghs have been fairly intensive since the mid-1970s. The burgh of Perth, as detailed above, has proved to contain remarkably well-preserved deposits and because of this has been used often to paint the picture of all Scotland's burghs. I have decided to tell the story of another burgh, St Andrews.

ST ANDREWS

> The boastful Frank, the war-loving Norman,
> the Flemish weaver and rough Teuton,
> English, German, Dutch, the man from Poitou with no knowledge of wool,
> and the blood-thirsty man from Anjou,
> those who drink the waters of Rhine and Rhone and the powerful Tiber come here to lay their prayers before Andrew.
> *Scotichronicon,* Walter Bower, 1440s

There is limited evidence for prehistoric occupation of the site now occupied by the town of St Andrews. Iron Age burials were found at Hallowhill and Kirkhill but no direct evidence of prehistoric settlement has yet been uncovered.

The first evidence for settlement is an entry in the Annals of Ulster dated AD 747. This states *MORS TUATHALAIN ABBATIS CINRIGHMONAI,* the death of Tuathal, Abbot of Cennrighmonaid. The place-name, variously spelt Cennrighmon-aid, Kilrimund, Kinrimund, means 'head of the king's mount', or if the Cenn is taken literally, 'church on the head of the king's mount'. The name is taken to refer to the headland above the harbour now known as Kirkhill.

The reference in the Annals of Ulster shows a unique interest in a distant Pictish religious house, particularly as the document was written in Ireland and not on Iona. The size and nature of the religious settlement referred to is not known but further clues are provided by the foundation legend of the settlement and finds from the cathedral precinct.

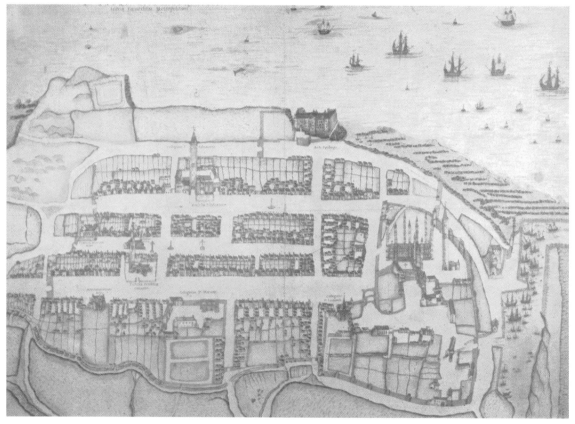

Geddy's Map of St Andrews 1580

The Cliffs at Kirkhill

The foundation legend tells that the boundary of the Pictish monastery was defined by free-standing crosses and records the building of seven churches within the monastic centre. Amongst the many early Christian sculpted stones recovered from the eastern half of the cathedral precinct was the shaft of a free-standing cross. This was found built into the eastern gable of the cathedral and is now on display in the site museum.

Many sculpted stones have been recovered: from Kirkhill, from St Mary's Church where they had been reused in the foundations, and during grave-digging operations in the cathedral precinct. These stones have no identifiable Pictish symbols and have been dated at the earliest to the late 9th and early 10th centuries. Two shrines have also been

St Mary of the Rock Church
Viewed from St Rule's Tower.
SUAT LTD

recovered from the cathedral precinct. The more impressive of the two, an elaborately decorated corner-post shrine, was found in the 19th century close to St Rule's Tower. The second, a solid stone shrine, was found 160 metres south-west of Kirkhill.

Although the land of Kinrimund is defined in 12th-century documents as covering 12.15 hectares, all the findspots of sculpted stones lie in an area of 4.05 hectares in the north-east corner of the cathedral precinct and on Kirkhill. Interestingly, this 4.05 hectares is similar to the areas enclosed by the boundaries of the monastic sites at Iona, and Clonmacnoise in Ireland.

Only one controlled modern archaeological excavation has taken place in this area. Radiocarbon dating of some of the human burials recovered suggested a date range between the 5th and 11th centuries AD, which suggests that some of the earlier burials relate to this religious centre.

Taken together, all the historical and archaeological evidence suggests that there was a major religious centre, possibly along Irish lines, on the headland at Kirkhill.

The early religious centre may have had an attached secular settlement. Again documentary evidence provides clues to its location and size. In a charter of 1189 Robert, bishop-elect, confirms the transfer of the market cross from the place where 'clochin' had been to the 'land of Lambinus'. It has been suggested that the word 'clochin' may be a corruption of the Gaelic word 'clachan' meaning a hamlet or kirktoun. Alternate views regarding the location of the 'clochin' have been expressed. Drs Nicholas Brooks and Graeme Whittington suggest that it occupied the eastern end of North Street and that the early market place occupied the part of North Street that fans out into a triangular area. Dr Ronald Cant suggests that North and South Castle Streets formed the main axis of the early settlement focusing on the castle. The other clue to the location of a pre-burgal secular settlement is the original location of the parish church of Holy Trinity. Until the 15th century it lay within the priory precinct to the south-east of the cathedral. The discovery of early structural evidence, apparently on a north to south axis, found during recent excavations at the site of the Byre Theatre in Abbey Street supports Cant's suggestion.

King David I gave permission for the founding of a burgh at St Andrews and granted the existing settlement to the bishop. This creation of an ecclesiastical burgh at St Andrews in 1140 marked a new phase. The erection of the cathedral appears to have obliterated the early religious centre and formed the focus of the new burgh. The new burgh was laid out on a diverging three-street plan and seems to have expanded westwards in stages. The planning and layout of the new burgh was under the control of Bishop Robert and Mainard the Fleming who was brought in specifically to lay it out (he had already performed the same function in Berwick-on-Tweed). Indeed, Mainard was made provost of the burgh and was given three landholdings in the town as a sign of gratitude. Brooks and Whittington suggest that the burgh had four stages of development between 1140 and the 15th or 16th century. The burgh limits in the 15th and 16th centuries are defined by the town ports and the location of the Franciscan and Dominican monasteries. The separate stages of development between the cathedral and the town ports are harder to define.

The central part of Market Street became the location of the burgh market around 1170 and a new market cross was erected. Recent excavations on Market Street seem to suggest that properties were laid out and occupied in the 12th and 13th centuries.

Medieval Corn-dryer
Sealed by deep garden soil, Market Street, St Andrews.
SUAT LTD

Leper Hospital

To the south of the burgh in the area now occupied by the East Sands Leisure Centre once stood the medieval leper hospital of St Nicholas. The first recorded reference to the hospital is in the 12th century. It still existed in the 16th century although by then it was referred to as 'a poor's hospital'. Excavation before the construction of the East Sands Leisure Centre found two of the leper hospital's boundary walls, and a stone building inside the hospital complex. This building appears to have been the hospital's bakehouse, as it contained a bread oven; it was substantially enlarged in the later phases of the building, possibly reflecting an increase in the number of patients. Although the hospital graveyard was not located in these excavations, some human bone was found; as this has proved to pre-date the hospital by some 400 years, it may indicate that an early graveyard existed on this site, perhaps influencing the choice of the site for the hospital. The site's proximity to the main pilgrim route from the crossing of the River Forth at Earlsferry is also significant, as the lepers would have been able to beg for alms from the passing pilgrims. The excavations at St Nicholas located a blocked-up doorway in the western boundary wall that may have been used as a 'begging gate'.

St Andrews appears always to have been of limited importance as an overseas trading port, in part due to the unsuitability of the harbour for large vessels. However, one of St Andrews' main industries was fishing, which required much smaller boats, and it is on record that the harbour was in use for this purpose from 1222.

The Exchequer Rolls show that goods from abroad had to be landed at Dundee and Inverkeithing then carried overland to the burgh. This apparent lack of direct involvement in overseas trade is reflected in the types of medieval pottery found by archaeologists – most pottery found was the local White Gritty Ware, with only a few sherds of imported pottery.

Because the burgh was founded around a (Catholic) religious centre, the fortunes of the burgh appear to have gone into a steep decline following the religious Reformation of 1559. This sudden change is reflected in the burgh's archaeology: on most sites within the burgh limits, identifiable medieval occupation ceases and is sealed by deep deposits of garden soil up to 1.5 metres thick. This probably reflects the turning over of the burgh backlands to intensive cultivation, presumably to provide food for the burgesses. In 1696, St Andrews University considered moving to the Gowrie House in Perth. The reason for this was partly because everyday items were expensive and there was a general lack of consumer goods such as shoes, clothes and hats, which had to be brought in from Edinburgh.

Contemporary 18th-century descriptions of St Andrews describe it as 'only a shadow of what it has been. The streets show grass as a pavement'. Dr Johnson in his famous account of a tour around Scotland describes St Andrews as a place 'which only history shows to have once flourished'.

Golf seems to have become the only expanding industry in St Andrews. The manufacture of leather-covered golf balls is recorded in the 18th century and in the 19th century, golf club manufacture became a thriving industry. Now golf and tourism form the major focal points of the town.

Because of its decline, the burgh's modern street plan retains much of the layout of the medieval burgh and a sensible conservation policy retains this element within the modern town.

The North-east and the Highlands

There has been limited archaeological work in the medieval burghs of the Highlands although excavations in Inverness have suggested that preservation in the core of the burgh may be very good. Elgin was the subject of some of the earliest urban archaeological excavations in Scotland, and Aberdeen has seen a great deal of excavation in the last 30 years.

ELGIN

> Elgin lies in 571/2 degrees north latitude, 2 degrees 25 minutes west longitude, being situated in the north-east quarter of that part of England commonly called Scotland.
> John Shanks, 1866

Elgin was founded as a royal burgh by David I in the 12th century. The successors of David I evidently viewed the burgh as an important centre of government, as William the Lion (1165–1214) granted 14 of his charters there. The establishment of the cathedral of the diocese of Moray at Elgin in 1224 also indicates the importance of the settlement at that date. It is only recently that modern development has begun to have a marked effect on the surviving medieval street plan.

The main street of the burgh, High Street, runs from east to west along a ridge, with the ground falling off to the north towards the River Lossie. The site of the royal castle lies on Ladyhill at the western end of the burgh, while the important cathedral and chanonry lie to the north-east.

It has become apparent from the archaeological work undertaken in Elgin that

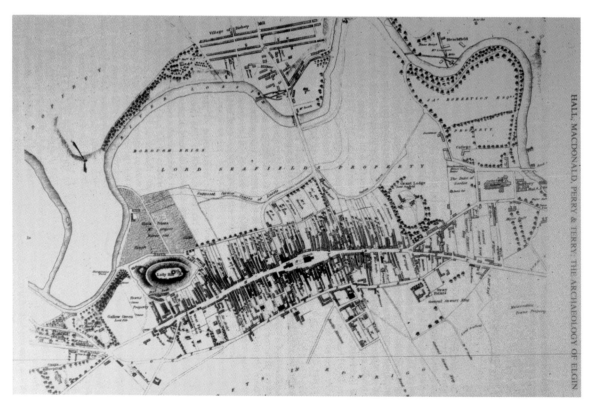

Wood's Map of Elgin, 1820

Aerial View of Elgin, Looking West

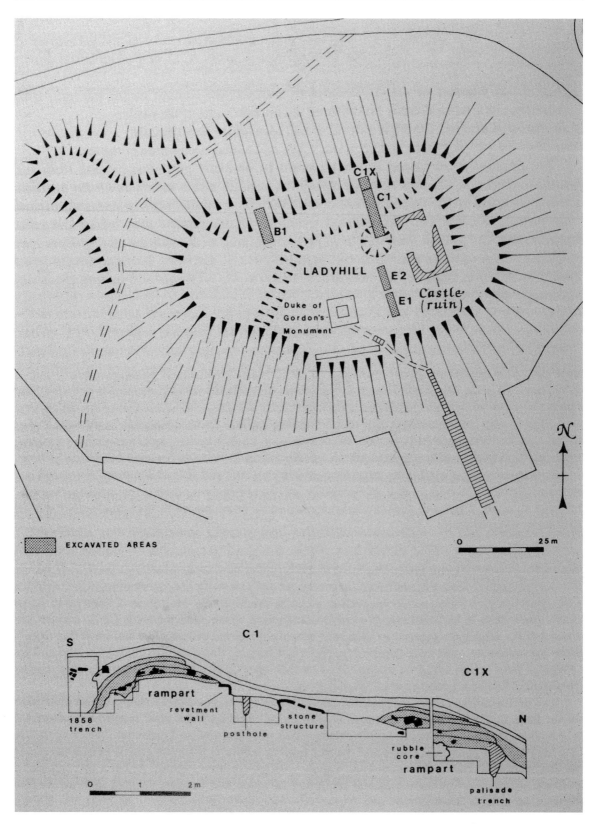

Excavations on Ladyhill, Elgin

SUAT LTD

The 'Elgin Pillar'
In the graveyard of Elgin Cathedral.

the location of the High Street on a ridge has an effect on the scale of preservation in the burgh. Limited observations at the west end of the High Street indicate that there may be no surviving deposits on the frontage: that is, each phase of building has in turn removed all traces of earlier structures. However, preservation in the backlands can be very good.

Prior to the building of the St Giles' Centre in 1988, the opportunity was taken to examine two sites close to the High Street frontage and St Giles' church. The well-preserved archaeological deposits survived only under the lines of former 'closes' (foot passages). It may be that any further deposits will only survive under such 'close' lines.

The accumulated evidence of excavation may suggest that the early burgh developed between the castle (on Ladyhill) and the church, then expanded eastwards towards the cathedral precincts in the 13th century. The early burgh may therefore have been concentrated closer to the castle in an area that is on the fringes of the modern town.

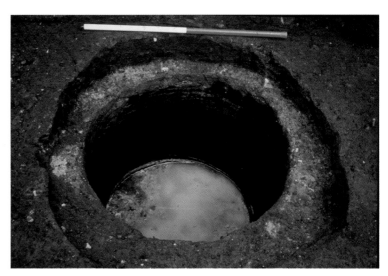

Barrel Well
From Nicholson's garage excavations, High Street, Elgin.
W J LINDSAY

Main Door of Elgin Cathedral
SUAT LTD

Conclusions

As the town in Scotland was very much a medieval invention, we know very little of what sorts of settlement, if any, existed before the times of David I. It seems very likely that most towns would have existed in some form before they gained their foundation charter. More evidence for this true dark age of Scotland would be greatly welcomed.

Since the beginning of urban archaeology in Scotland in the mid-1970s a vast amount of information about the lives of the everyday people of medieval Scotland has been recovered. Together with the evidence from documents we can reconstruct much of the lives of the burgesses and other townspeople. What have we learned?

Perhaps one of the most striking things is how much closer the people of continental Europe seem to have been to the inhabitants of medieval Scotland. Although few people would ever have been able to travel to these places, there were constant contacts with foreign merchants and traders, who must have been common visitors to Scottish shores.

Religion clearly played a much greater part in people's lives than it does nowadays: the friars of the different monastic orders would have been a common sight on the streets of the medieval burgh. It is the important link that these establishments had to the burgh as a whole that makes their excavation so interesting. They cannot be viewed in isolation from the community of the burgh.

Perth High Street Excavations
General view.
SUAT LTD

One of the most striking things about towns like Perth is the depth and quality of the surviving archaeology – there is little to match the feeling of standing on the surface of the medieval High Street and looking up some 3 or 4 metres to the modern one. Although we have a unique resource in the archaeological deposits of Perth, as a thriving, cosmopolitan market and trading centre the town would have been subject to different influences and contacts from small burghs in the back of beyond. We certainly need to know more about the smaller burghs, further away from the focus of trade and foreign influence. Investigation of a burgh such as Clackmannan, for example, would give us a clearer idea of what life in a 'normal' burgh was like.

Most urban archaeology has been driven by the need to dig and record the medieval layers before they are destroyed by development, rather than by carefully directed research to answer questions about the important towns. This makes the work of Charlie and Hillary Murray at the deserted burgh of Rattray in Aberdeenshire very important; but perhaps we should be doing more to explore the histories of the burghs of Scotland.

If this book has succeeded in offering some tantalising glimpses of what we know about our past through urban archaeology, then hopefully it might help people to appreciate the value of our archaeological deposits and ensure that they are properly looked after.

Buildings and Blacksmith's Workshop
Reconstructed view, Meal Vennel, Perth.
SUAT LTD

Sites to Visit in Scotland

This section has picked those Scottish burghs which still retain some of their medieval character and either contain standing buildings, distinctive street plans or museums with good displayed collections of excavated material. Some of the sites mentioned are opened to the public by Historic Scotland (HS) or other agencies (P), but many are in private ownership and permission should be sought from the owner before making a visit. The burghs are listed alphabetically in local authority areas.

City of Dundee

Dundee

Despite the extensive redevelopment of the 1960s Dundee still retains some elements of its medieval past. These are probably best represented by the church of St Mary in the Nethergate (P) and its modern street plan, particularly around the axis of the Murraygait and Seagait.

East Lothian

Haddington

Although the place name Haddington is of Anglian origin little or nothing is known of any settlement at this period. The town first makes its appearance as a Royal burgh in the reign of David I in a charter of 1147x1153. It is believed that the Burgh grew up around the High Street, a continuation of the road from Edinburgh, which originally formed a wide, open market area. Some time before 1425 buildings were erected in the centre of the market place, and this had the effect of creating two streets, Market Street to the north and High Street to the south. Because of its position between Edinburgh and the border, Haddington was burned by English armies on three occasions, in 1213, 1241 and 1333. The town was also flooded in 1385. In 1547–8 the town was fortified by the English. The burgh still retains much of its medieval character particularly in its street layout and bridge across the River to the suburb of Nungate.

Fife

St Andrews

Widely noted for its cathedral, university and latterly its golfing facilities, St Andrews has nevertheless remained throughout its long history a fairly compact and self contained town. The original settlement, which was situated between the Kinness Burn and the sea, was a Culdee community which became the primary religious centre of the kingdom of Scotia. The Culdees were gradually assimilated by the Augustinians after the priory and cathedral church were founded in 1144 (HS). St Andrews was founded before 1144 as a non-royal burgh by Bishop Robert (1121–59) by leave of King David I. Although not a royal burgh until 1620, it attended the general council in 1357 and was active in Parliament from 1456. Slowly, by stages, the town expanded westward, and by the 16th century had reached the limits defined by ports at South Street, Market Street and North Street. The medieval town layout of St. Andrews is today still virtually intact. Kinburn House Museum contains an important displayed collection of excavated artefacts from the excavations described in the relevant section of this book.

Highland

Inverness

Inverness is assumed to have been one of David I's burghs. The early burgh is thought to have grown up near the base of the castle hill and then extended down towards the church. By the later Middle Ages the four principal streets of the burgh formed a cross at the base of Castle hill, a pattern which still survives today. A river crossing to the north of the burgh at Friar Shotts may have given greater prominence to the northern part of the burgh during its early development, with Church Street (formerly Kirkgate) being the major axis of the burgh until the construction of a bridge across the Ness in the 13th century. The emphasis then shifted from Church Street onto the High Street (then called Eastgate). The medieval town was defended by a ditch and palisade, and remained mostly within the confines of these defences until the 19th century, except for a medieval suburb at Eastgate.

Moray

Elgin

Elgin was founded as a royal burgh by David I in the 12th century. The successors of David I evidently viewed the burgh as an important centre of government, as William the Lion (1165–1214) granted fourteen of his charters there. The establishment of the cathedral of the diocese of Moray at Elgin in 1224 also indicates the importance of the settlement at that date. It is only recently that modern development has begun to have a marked effect on the surviving medieval street plan. It still retains its distinctive 'cigar' shaped High Street and the cathedral, once known as the 'Lantern of the North', still remains an impressive monument well worthy of a visit (HS). Elgin museum has some of the excavated medieval artefacts from the Relief road excavations of the 1970s on display (P).

North Ayrshire

Ayr

There appears to have been a settlement or at least a castle at Ayr prior to its foundation as a royal burgh in the early 13th century. It has been convincingly argued that this pre-charter settlement was located along the

Sandgate It also seems to be the reason for the duplication of the many important burgh buildings such as tolbooths and market crosses. Ayr possesses the earliest surviving charter of erection of any royal burgh in Scotland. The tower of the former medieval parish church of St John still survives (P) and the medieval 'Old Brig' still stands across the River Ayr.

Perth and Kinross

Perth

The burgh of Perth retains very little of medieval date except for the very important church of St John whose tower probably dates to the 14th century. Its basic medieval gridded street pattern remains despite much redevelopment in the town centre. Perth museum displays an important collection of excavated artefacts in its rotunda the remnants of a once larger exhibition called 'Medieval muck and Middens' (P).

Stirling

The burgh of Stirling lies near the mid-point of the central belt of Scotland, at the eastern end of the Carse of Forth, between the Highland hills to the North and the Lowland (Gargunnock) hills to the south-west. The River Forth was navigable to Stirling until the end of the 19th century.

Rather like Edinburgh, the old town of Stirling developed in the lee of the castle, on the slope

forming the main approach to the Castle Rock. But whereas the old town of Edinburgh stands on a 'tail' of glacial debris, Stirling stands on a ridge of volcanic rock extending to the south of the castle. Bedrock outcrops are visible in several parts of the burgh and in other places it is close to modern ground level. This makes the prediction of archaeological preservation very difficult. However recent work has indicated that deep anaerobic midden deposits do survive in clefts in this bedrock.

Until the creation of new roads around the bottom of the volcanic outcrop in the mid-19th century, anyone travelling from the south of Scotland to the north had to go through Stirling itself. In medieval times, most of the surrounding area was impassable carse land, dissected by the sinuous course of the Forth and its tributaries. All routes converged on the only practicable crossing of the Forth, totally dominated by the almost impregnable Castle Rock, making Stirling the key to the whole realm of Scotland. The surviving medieval and late-medieval buildings of Cowans hospital (P), Argylls Lodging (HS), the church of the Holy Rude (P) and the castle give the Old town a medieval flavour (HS). The Smith Museum and Art Gallery contains some of the medieval artefacts found in the burgh (P).

Further Reading

Conservation and Change in Historic Towns, edited by E Patricia Dennison (Council for British Archaeology Research Report 122 1999)

Townlife in Fourteenth-Century Scotland, Elizabeth Ewan (Edinburgh University Press 1990)

Excavations in the Medieval Burgh of Perth 1979–81, edited by Philip Holdsworth (Society of Antiquaries of Scotland Monograph 5 1987)

The Scottish Medieval Town, edited by Michael Lynch, Michael Spearman and Geoffrey Stell (John Donald 1988)

Excavations in Medieval St Andrews 1980–89: A decade of archaeology, edited by Mike Rains and Derek Hall (Tayside and Fife Archaeological Committee Monograph 1 1997)

A Tale of Two Burghs, Judith Stones (Aberdeen Art Gallery and Museums 1987)

Medieval Scotland, Peter Yeoman (Batsford/Historic Scotland 1995)

Acknowledgements

This book reflects the hard work of many Scottish urban archaeologists over the last 25 or so years. I would particularly like to acknowledge the skill and dedication of the staff of SUAT Ltd on whose work much of this book is based. I would also like to acknowledge the support and interest of Gordon Barclay of Historic Scotland and Hugh Andrew of Birlinn. This book is dedicated to Alice, Kitty and Fergus.

HISTORIC SCOTLAND

HISTORIC SCOTLAND safeguards Scotland's built heritage, including its archaeology, and promotes its understanding and enjoyment on behalf of the Secretary of State for Scotland. It undertakes a programme of 'rescue archaeology', from which many of the results are published in this book series.

Scotland has a wealth of ancient monuments and historic buildings, ranging from prehistoric tombs and settlements to remains from the Second World War, and HISTORIC SCOTLAND gives legal protection to the most important, guarding them against damaging changes or destruction. HISTORIC SCOTLAND gives grants and advice to the owners and occupiers of these sites and buildings.

HISTORIC SCOTLAND has a membership scheme which allows access to properties in its care, as well as other benefits.

For information, contact:
0131 668 8999.